Indonesian
phrasebook

Paul Woods
Kristiana Sarwo Rini
Margit Meinhold

Indonesian Phrasebook
2nd edition

Published by
Lonely Planet Publications
Head Office: PO Box 617, Hawthorn, Vic 3122, Australia
Branches: PO Box 2001A, Berkeley, CA 94702, USA and London, UK

Printed by
Colorcraft Ltd, Hong Kong

Published
August 1992

About This Book
This edition was written by Paul Woods, with assistance from Kristiana
Sarwo Rini. The 1st edition was written by Margit Meinhold. Sally Steward
edited the book, Tamsin Wilson was responsible for cover and illustrations,
and Glenn Beanland for design.

National Library of Australia Cataloguing in Publication Data

Woods, Paul
    Indonesian Phrasebook

    2nd ed.
    ISBN 0 86442 147 8

    1. Indonesian language – Conversation and phrase books – English. I.
    Meinhold, Margit. Indonesia phrasebook. II. Title. (Series: Language
    survival kit).

499.22183421
© Copyright Lonely Planet 1992

Contents

Introduction

Indonesian, or Bahasa Indonesia as it is more correctly called, is the lingua franca of Indonesia. It was first used formally by nationalists Sukarno and Mohammed Hatta to write the declaration of Indonesian independence in August 1945. The language was a symbol of unity and nationalism at that time, and was later adopted as the national language of education and government throughout Indonesia. There are, however, over 300 different languages spoken throughout Indonesia, so you'll find most people use their own local language, *bahasa daerah*, at home and Bahasa Indonesia to communicate with visitors. Most people you meet in Indonesia (with the exception of Irian Jaya) will speak Bahasa Indonesia well – it is usually only the older people and preschool children who are not fluent. Jakarta, as the melting pot of Indonesia, has even developed its own characteristic dialect, called *Bahasa Betawi*, from the old Dutch name for the capital of the Dutch East Indies, 'Batavia'.

Bahasa Indonesia is derived from Malay, which was used for many centuries as the language of traders who plied the Indonesian archipeligo. These included Arabs, Chinese, Portuguese and Dutch, whose languages have all left their legacy in today's Bahasa Indonesia. It is a very dynamic language and is constantly absorbing new vocabulary, more recent influences including English, which is now the most popular foreign language.

One of the best aspects of travelling in Indonesia and learning Indonesian is that even your most stumbling attempts in the language will be greeted with enthusiasm. Just a few words spoken will be rewarded with the exclamation *'Wah, sudah lancar bahasa Indonesianya'*, which is a compliment on your fluency.

What is important and appreciated is your attempt, rather than your ability. This has got to be one of the reasons why so many people pick up a reasonable ability to communicate in only a few weeks' stay in Indonesia, and get a great deal of enjoyment in the process.

Bahasa Indonesia (literally 'language of Indonesia') is an easy language to pick up for the purpose of everyday communication. There are, however, a few points to note. To be able to read and write Bahasa Indonesia well takes a long period of study, just like any other language, because of the use of complex grammar which is not used in everyday speech, and the fact that formal writings contain a far greater range of vocabulary than is used in speaking. So don't expect to be able to read the newspaper after one month in Indonesia.

Everyday speech is a very simplified form of the language, which is a great plus for beginners, however you'll find that people communicate with each other at such a machinegun speed that you'll be left well behind. This is why you'll need to master *'Maaf, Bahasa Indonesia saya belum lancar'*, which means 'I'm not yet fluent in Indonesian', in order to avoid being overwhelmed by a burst of local dialect.

This phrasebook has been designed to enable you to travel independently in Indonesia. It is an invaluable companion to the comprehensive guidebook, *Indonesia: a travel survival kit*, also published by Lonely Planet.

Selamat jalan! – Bon voyage!

Pronunciation

Indonesian is a very easy language to learn, and even easier to pronounce. Each single letter represents a sound. With a couple of exceptions, the sounds are the same every time and receive equal emphasis. Generally, the last syllable in a word is stressed, and in sentences, stress is on the most important word.

Vowels

a like the 'u' in 'hut' or 'up'

Apa kabar?	How are you?
Kabar baik.	Fine thanks.

e a short sound, like the 'e' in 'open', when it is unstressed, in which case it is hardly pronounced at all, or like the 'e' in 'café' when it is stressed. A stressed **e** at the end of a word is a little longer, but the stress can also fall on other syllables.

Selamat sore.	'slamat soray'	Good afternoon.
meja	'mayja'	table
merdeka	'merdayka'	free

i like the 'i' in 'unique'. The length of the sound doesn't alter.

Selamat tidur.	'slamat tidur'	Good night.
Selamat tinggal.	'slamat ting gal'	Farewell.

o similar to the English 'o' sound in either 'hot' or 'cold'. Generally speaking you won't be misunderstood if you pronounce this sound as you would in English.

foto	photograph
obat	medicine

u	as the 'oo' in 'too', only shorter		
	satu	'satoo'	one
	dua	'doo-a'	two

Diphthongs

There are also three vowel combinations: **ai**, **au** and **ua**. The sounds of the individual vowels do not change, they are simply run on by sliding from one to the other.

| **ai** | sounds like 'i' in 'like' | | |
| | *Kabar baik.* | 'kabar bai' | I'm fine. |

au	sounds like a drawn out 'ow' like 'cow'		
	saudara	'sowdara'	you (or brother)
	mau	as in Chairman 'Mao'	want

ua	begins with the sound of 'oo' as in 'too' and ends with the 'ah' sound in 'hut'		
	uang	'ooahng'	money
	puas	'pooahs'	satisfied

Consonants

The pronunciation of consonants is very straightforward. Each is pronounced consistently, and most sound like English consonants.

| **b** | always pronounced as the 'b' in 'rub' | | |
| | *bagi* | 'bagi' | for |

| **p** | always pronounced as the 'p' in 'lip' | | |
| | *panas* | 'panas' | hot |

| **c** | always pronounced 'ch' as in 'chair' | | |
| | *karcis* | 'karchis' | ticket |

| **g** | always pronounced hard, as the 'g' in 'garden' | | |
| | *pagi* | 'pagi' | morning |

ng	always pronounced as the 'ng' in 'sing'		
	siang	'siang'	day
	tinggal	'ting gal'	live

j   pronounced as 'dj'. It's the sound you hear at the beginning of 'join'.

tujuh	'tudjuh'	seven

r   pronounced very clearly and distinctly. It is always slightly trilled.

Apa kabar?	'apa kabarrr'	How are you?
Selamat tidur.	'slamat tidurrr'	Good night.

h   always pronounced, except at the end of a word. It is stressed a little more strongly than in English, as if you were sighing. This heavy pronunciation is particularly true for words of Arabic origin, when the 'h' appears between two vowels which are the same.

hotel	'hhotel'	hotel
mahal	'mahhhal'	expensive
rupiah	'rupia'	local currency

k pronounced the same as the English 'k', unless it appears at the end of a word, when you should stop just short of actually saying the 'k'.

　　Kabar baik.　　'kabar bai'　　　　I'm well.

ny a single sound, like the 'ny' in 'canyon' or the beginning of 'new', before the 'oo' part of the word.

　　nyonya　　　　'nyonya'　　　　Mrs

Grammar

Indonesian grammar is simple to master for the purpose of basic communication. Nouns do not have plural forms, the pattern of sentences is straightforward, and sentences are usually short.

Word Order

The word order for Indonesian sentences is the same as for English sentences: subject, verb, object. The simplest sentence structure of 'subject, verb, object' can be illustrated with *Saya membaca buku*, literally 'I reading book': 'I am reading a book'.

It is quite common in Indonesian for the object to be mentioned first. This however requires modification of the verb form and so it is easier as a beginner in Indonesian to simply use the subject-verb-object construction illustrated above.

There are no special terms for 'is' and 'are', and there are no articles, 'a' and 'the'. Thus *Buku merah*, literally 'book red', means 'The book is red'.

For sentences where no subject is obvious, the word *ada* is used. *Ada* is the nearest equivalent to 'there is', but means 'to be' in the sense of 'to exist'. *Ada buku merah*, for example, means 'There is a red book'. It may also be used to indicate possession, for example *Saya ada uang*, which means 'I have money'.

Verbs

Indonesian has a basic verb form which may be used in colloquial speech, and you will be understood perfectly well when you use it. You will notice however, that in more formal situations and for use in written communication, there is a system of prefixes which are added to the root word. The correct prefix depends on the type of verb and its context in the sentence. There are basically three types or classes of verbs. The simplest type stands alone and never requires a prefix, when used as a verb. Fortunately many of the most commonly used verbs fit into this category:

to sit	*duduk*
to eat	*makan*
to drink	*minum*
to cook	*masak*
to bathe	*mandi*
to go	*pergi*
to want	mau
to know	tahu

The second category is the 'ber verbs', because *ber* is used as a prefix to the root word. For example, the root word *bicara,* becomes *berbicara,* 'to speak'. 'Ber verbs' are quite common:

to ask	*bertanya*
to play	*bermain*
to swim	*berenang*

The third category is verbs which use the *me* prefix. Note that the prefix varies a little from word to word, and the root word is sometimes modified, so that, for instance, the root word for 'read', *tulis,* becomes *menulis:*

to read	*membaca*
to write	*menulis*
to answer	*menjawab*
to buy	*membeli*
to open	*membuka*
to search	*mencari*
to assist	*membantu*

The correct use of prefixes with verbs takes a long time to master, and there are other forms of verbs as well as those mentioned here, but remember that in everyday speech the use of the root word alone will nevertheless convey a clear meaning.

Tense

Verbs do not change their form with tense. Tense can be denoted by context, such as the insertion of a time word such as *besok,* 'tomorrow', and *kemarin,* 'yesterday', anywhere in the sentence. For example *Saya membeli mobil kemarin* means 'I bought a car yesterday', while *Saya mau membeli mobil besok* means 'I will buy a car tomorrow'.

Alternatively, there are several special tense indicators which are always placed immediately before the verb in a sentence. The most common are *sudah*, *sedang* and *akan* which denote past, present and future tenses, respectively. For example *Saya sudah makan* means 'I have already eaten', *Saya sedang makan* means 'I'm still eating' and *Saya akan makan*, meaning 'I will eat', shows that the action is in the future. For an action which has very recently taken place we can use *baru saja*: *Saya baru saja makan* 'I have just finished eating'.

To illustrate sentence construction and the use of verbs, here are a few examples:

to eat	*makan*
The man eats chicken.	*Orang itu makan ayam.*
to drink	*minum*
I want to drink tea.	*Saya mau minum teh.*
to want	*mau*
They want to sleep.	*Mereka mau tidur.*
to go	*pergi*
The children go to the shop.	*Anak-anak pergi ke toko.*

Adjectives

Adjectives follow the noun:

red book	*buku merah*
this book	*buku ini*
my book	*buku saya*
big house	*rumah besar*

When you want to say more than one thing about the noun you use '... *yang* ...':

the small red book	*buku merah yang kecil*
	'book small which red'
the big white house	*rumah putih yang besar*
	'house white which big'

Comparisons in Indonesian are made with the use of *lebih*, 'more' and *kurang*, 'less' – both placed before the adjective. *Daripada* is also used in the place of 'than' in English, if both objects being compared are specifically mentioned. For example *Mangga lebih mahal daripada pisang*, 'Mangoes are more expensive than bananas'.

bigger than	*lebih besar daripada*
	'more big than'
smaller than	*lebih kecil daripada*
	'more small than'
more delicious than	*lebih enak daripada*
fewer than	*kurang banyak daripada*
more than	*lebih banyak daripada*

To indicate extremes of comparison, *paling* is used:

the biggest shop	*toko yang paling besar*
the smallest shop	*toko yang paling kecil*
cheapest	*paling murah*
the most expensive	*paling mahal*
The bigger hotel is the most expensive.	*Hotel yang lebih besar paling mahal.*

The smaller car is the cheapest.

Mobil yang lebih kecil paling murah.

Personal Pronouns

Personal pronouns reflect levels of politeness, so that *saudara*, 'you', (literally: 'brother'), is the more formal version of *kamu*, 'you'. *Kamu* is used only with friends. The word *anda* also means

'you', and is acceptable in most situations. It is better to use this as a polite form, rather than *saudara*, which is rarely used in everyday speech. *Bapak* or *Pak* (literally: 'father') and *Ibu* or *Bu* (literally: 'mother') are commonly used respectful terms for an older man or woman.

The second person plural, 'we', also has two versions: *kita*, 'we', including the person spoken to; and *kami*, which only includes the people spoken about and not the person being addressed.

I/my	*saya*
you (sg)	(*kamu*)or *anda* [*saudara*]
he/she	*ia* or *dia*
we	*kami* or *kita*
you (pl)	*saudara sekalian* or *anda*
they	*mereka*

Possession

The personal pronouns are used to indicate possession. They are unchanged and placed after the noun.

my jacket	*jaket saya*
your ticket	*karcis saudara*
Mina's hotel	*hotel Mina*

An alternative way of indicating possession, which should only be used for the third person (he, she or they), is the suffix *nya*:

his jacket	*jaketnya*
their money	*uangnya*

Questions

The structure of question sentences is not difficult to master. You can make a question by simply raising the pitch of your voice at the end of the sentence.

There are a number of question words you may want to use as well. These are put at the beginning of the sentence:

what
How are you?

apa
Apa kabar?
'what news?'

who
What is your name?

siapa anda (Gnl)
Siapa nama kamu? (inf)
'who name you?'

when
When does the bus go?

kapan
Kapan bis pergi?

where
Where is the station?

dimana
Dimana stasiun?

from where
Where did you come from?

darimana
Darimana?

to where
Where does the bus go to?

kemana
Kemana bis pergi?

how/in what way
How do we eat?

bagaimana
Bagaimana kita makan?

how much/many
How much is this?

berapa price
Berapa harga ini?

why
Why is the bus late?

mengapa
Mengapa bis terlambat?

may I?
May I come in?

boleh?
Boleh saya masuk?

A third possible way to make a question is by the addition of *kah* to the end of the most important word, that is, the word the question is about. You may wish to make use of this when you have acquired a certain level of proficiency. You can certainly get by without it.

Negation

Tidak and *bukan* are used to indicate negation. Both mean 'not' or 'no'. *Tidak* is put in front of verbs and adjectives, and *bukan* is put in front of nouns:

I do not want it.	*Saya tidak mau.*
This is not a book.	*Ini bukan buku.*

Both words can be used on their own to mean 'No' in answer to a question.

Plurals

The same word is used for singular or plural. There are no endings in Indonesian which may be attached to a word to make it plural. Generally the context will indicate whether something is plural or not. For example *banyak orang* means 'many people'. In writing, the noun is repeated to indicate plural:

child	*anak*
children	*anak-anak*

Doubling a word has several other functions. It can sometimes intensify the actual meaning of the word.

slow	*pelan*
slowly	*pelan-pelan*
sit	*duduk*
sitting around	*duduk-duduk*

Because of this potential for confusion it's probably best to avoid indiscriminate doubling. Quantity can be indicated by a number, or a quantity word placed before the noun.

Quantity Words

all	*semua*
both	*keduanya*
each	*tiap-tiap*
enough	*cukup*
every	*masing-masing*
little	*sedikit*
many/much	*banyak*
some	*beberapa*

These quantity words always precede the noun they qualify:

| There are many people. | *Banyak orang.* |

Other Useful Words
Adverbs

always	*selalu*
also	*juga*
immediately	*dengan segara*
never	*tak pernah*
not yet	*belum*
often	*sering*

perhaps	*barangkali*
possibly	*mungkin*
rather	*agak*
really	*sungguh*
too	*terlalu*
very	*sekali*

Conjunctions

after	*sesudah*
as soon as	*segara*
because	*karena*
before	*sebelum*
if	*kalau*
or	*atau*
since	*sejak*
when	*waktu*
while	*sedang*

Prepositions

about	*tentang*
at, in, on (place)	*di*
at, in (time)	*pada*
between	*antara*
during	*selama*
for	*untuk*
from	*dari*
since	*sejak*
through	*melalui*
till	*sampai*
to	*ke*
with	*dengan*
without	*tanpa*

Greetings & Civilities

People in Indonesia put more emphasis on politeness and civilities than you may be accustomed to, so you will be accepted much better if you use the common civilities.

Greetings
In English we can say 'Good morning' or 'Good evening' or 'Good day', depending on the time of day. It's the same in Indonesian.

Good morning. (7 – 11 am)	*Selamat pagi.*
Good day. (11 am – 3 pm)	*Selamat siang.*
Good afternoon. (3 – 7 pm)	*Selamat sore.*
Good evening. (after dark)	*Selamat malam.*
Good night. (on retiring)	*Selamat tidur.*

Civilities
For Indonesians it is a sign of polite restraint not to accept an offer when it is first made. Therefore, if you are offering somebody something don't be deterred by their first refusal. Repeat the offer and it will probably be accepted.

When you are visiting somebody in their house you will be served a sweet drink which is sometimes accompanied by a snack.

If it is not to your liking, it is quite acceptable to take just a few sips. If you don't want to take the snack, just say *Maaf, saya masih kenyang*, meaning 'Sorry, I have just eaten.' (literally: I am still satisfied).

Enjoy your meal.	*Selamat makan.*
Enjoy your drink.	*Selamat minum.*
Farewell.	*Selamat tinggal.*
(when you are leaving)	
Farewell.	*Selamat jalan.*
(to someone, when you are staying)	
Welcome.	*Selamat datang.*
See you later.	*Sampai jumpa lagi.*

Selamat, which means 'May your action be blessed', comes from the Arabic word, *salam*. Putting this word together with 'morning' or 'evening' then translates into something like 'Have a nice morning/evening'. All sorts of actions may be blessed, and *selamat* is a word you will hear quite often.

In Indonesian there are two words for 'please'. *Tolong* is used when you are making a request or when you are asking somebody to do something for you. If you are offering something to somebody you use *silahkan*. For example:

please/help	*tolong*
Please shut the door.	*Tolong tutup pintu itu.*
Please clean my room.	*Tolong bersihkan kamar saya.*
Please come in.	*Silahkan masuk.*
Please sit down.	*Silahkan duduk.*

Although people appreciate politeness, you will find that 'thank you' is used less frequently than in English.

Thank you.	*Terima kasih.*
You're welcome.	*Kembali.*
You're welcome. (colloquial)	*Sama-sama.*
Excuse me.	*Permisi.*
Pardon? (What did you say?)	*Ma'af?*
I'm sorry … (apology)	*Ma'af…*

Forms of Address

In Indonesia you will hear two forms of address. The most usual is the *Bu/Pak* combination. These words literally mean 'Mother' and 'Father'. They are also used in situations which require a greater show of respect or a greater degree of formality, as in a passport office, for instance. *Saudara* literally means 'brother' or 'sister' and it can be used to mean 'you', which shows a degree of respect, but *anda* is now more commonly used. When talking to children you may want to use *kamu* or *dik*, from the word 'adik' meaning younger brother or sister.

Mr	*Bapak, Pak*
Mrs	*Ibu, Bu*
Miss	*Nona*

Body Language

Shaking hands in Indonesia involves only a light brief touch of the hand, and is suitable for both men and women. It is appropriate to shake hands when being introduced to somebody, when visiting somebody in their house, or when you haven't seen somebody for a while.

It is considered polite to bow your body slightly when walking across in front of somebody who is seated. At the same time you can say *permisi*, which just means 'excuse me'.

Standing with your hands on your hips is considered to be a sign of anger or aggression and therefore should be avoided.

Small Talk

As you travel around Indonesia you will be meeting people and wanting to make conversation. You will almost certainly be asked questions about yourself and the members of your family.

Meeting People

What is your name?	*Siapa nama anda?*
My name is …	*Nama saya …*

Nationalities

Where are you from?	*Dari mana?*
I am from …	*Saya dari …*
Australia	*Australia*
Canada	*Kanada*
England	*Inggris*
Europe	*Eropa*
Ireland	*Irlandia*
Japan	*Jepang*
New Zealand	*Zealandia Baru*
Scotland	*Skotlandia*
the USA	*Amerika*
I am …	*Saya …*
Australian	*orang Australia*
American	*orang Amerika*
British	*orang Inggeris*
Canadian	*orang Kanada*
Dutch	*orang Belanda*

English	*orang Inggeris*
foreigner	*orang asing*
Irish	*orang Irlandia*
New Zealander	*orang Zealandia Baru*

Age

How old are you?	*Umur anda berapa?*
I am …	*Saya …*
20 years old	*dua puluh tahun*
35 years old	*tiga puluh lima tahun*

Occupations

What is your occupation?	*Pekerjaan anda apa?*
(I am a/an …)	
artist	*seniman*
businessperson	*pengusaha*
doctor	*dokter*
engineer	*insinyur*
factory worker	*pekerja pabrik*
farmer	*petani*
journalist	*wartawan*
lawyer	*ahli hukum*
mechanic	*montir*
musician	*pemain musik*
nurse	*perawat*
public servant	*pegawai negeri*
sailor	*pelaut*
singer	*penyanyi*
scientist	*ahli sains*
secretary	*sekertaris*
student	*siswa*
teacher	*guru*
writer	*penulis*

Religion

What is your religion?	*Agama anda apa?*
My religion is …	*Agama saya …*
Buddhist	*Budha*
Catholic	*Katolik*
Christian	*Kristen*
Hindu	*Hindu*

| Jewish | *Yehudi* |
| Muslim | *Islam* |

Most Indonesians are Muslim, some are Christian, a few are Hindu and Buddhist. Indonesians may feel uncomfortable if you do not profess a religion, often equating atheism with communism. Therefore, you will maintain better relations by claiming to have a religion.

Family

This is my ...	*Ini ... saya*
mother	*ibu*
father	*bapak*
older sister/brother	*kakak*
younger brother/sister	*adik*
child	*anak*
children	*anak-anak*
son	*anak laki-laki*
daughter	*perempuan*
husband	*suami*
wife	*istri*
friend	*teman*

Questions about you and your life will be asked quite frequently, in particular, *Sudah kawin?*, 'Are you already married?'. Unless you are indeed married, the appropriate answer is *Belum!*, 'Not yet!'

Tidak, 'No', would be grammatically fine to use, but most Indonesians would not understand why you should not be married or not thinking about it. You will get on a lot better, especially if you are a woman, if you answer *Sudah* or *Belum*.

already	*sudah*
not yet	*belum*
no	*tidak*

Are you married?	*Sudah kawin?*
I am not married yet.	*Saya belum kawin.*
I am married.	*Saya sudah kawin.*
Do you have any children?	*Punya anak?*
I do not have any children.	*Saya tidak punya.*

I have ...	*Saya punya ...*
one son	*satu anak laki-laki*
one daughter	*satu anak perempuan*
three sons	*tiga anak laki-laki*
three daughters	*tiga anak perempuan*
How many brothers and sisters do you have?	*Berapa saudara anda?*
Do you have a boyfriend/ girlfriend?	*Punya pacar?*

Feelings

I am ...	*Saya ...*
angry	*marah*
bored	*bosan*
cold	*dingin*
full	*kenyang*
happy	*senang*
hot	*panas*
hungry	*laparad*
in a hurry	*terburu-buru*
sad	*sedih*
scared	*takut*
sick	*sakit*
thirsty	*haus*
tired	*lelah*

Language Problems

Do you speak English?	*Bisa berbicara bahasa Inggris?*
Yes, I do.	*Bisa.*
No, I do not.	*Tidak bisa.*

Can (handwritten)

I only know a little Indonesian.	*Saya hanya tahu sedikit bahasa Indonesia.*
Does any one here speak English?	*Ada orang disini yang bisa bahasa Inggris?*
Do you understand?	*Mengerti?*
I don't understand.	*Saya tidak mengerti.*
How do you say … in Indonesian?	*Apa bahasa Indonesianya …?*
What does this mean?	*Apa artinya?*
Please speak slowly!	*Bisa bicara lebih lambat.*
Write that word down for me.	*Tolong tuliskan kata itu.*
Please repeat it.	*Tolong ulangi.*
Please translate for me.	*Tolong terjemahkan.*

Interests

What is your hobby?	*Apa hobi anda?*
I like …	*Saya suka …*
I do not like …	*Saya tidak suka …*
discos	*disko*
film	*filem*
going shopping	*berbelanja*
music	*musik*
playing games	*bermain game*
playing sport	*berolahraga*
reading books	*membaca buku*
travelling	*berjalan-jalan*
watching TV	*nonton televisi*

Some Useful Phrases

Look!	*Lihat!*
Listen!	*Dengarlah!*
I am ready.	*Saya siap.*
Slow down!	*Pelan-pelan!*
Hurry up!	*Cepat-cepat!*
Go away!	*Pergi!*
Watch out!	*Awas!*
It is possible.	*Mungkin.*
It is not possible.	*Tidak mungkin.*
I forgot.	*Saya lupa.*
It is important.	*Penting.*
It is not important.	*Tidak penting.*
Where are you going?	*Mau kemana?*
What is this called?	*Apa ini?*
Can I take a photo?	*Boleh saya potret?*
Do you live here?	*Tinggal di sini?*

Getting Around

Travelling in Indonesia is a slow business, so you don't want to be in a hurry. Departure times are usually approximate, although this is not always so. A lot of projects are underway to improve the condition of the roads but this work is done by manual labour and takes time, so long-distance travel on those bumpy roads can be tedious and uncomfortable. Buses and bemos are usually overcrowded, so if it's at all possible organise yourself to sit in the middle, but not over the wheel, and avoid sitting next to the driver as the gear changes will ruin your kneecaps. If the price is not posted up somewhere, as it usually is for sea travel, you may bargain for a reduction of the fare. If the ticket counter is closed, the head of the bus station or boat office will help you.

Finding Your Way

Where is the ...?	*Dimana ... ?*
city bus station	*terminal bis kota*
city bus stop	*halte bis kota*
inter-city bus station	*terminal bis (antar kota)*
train station	*setasiun kereta api*
airport	*lapangan terbang*

What time does the ... leave?	*Jam berapa ... berangkat?*
city bus	*bis kota*
inter-city bus	*bis (antar kota)*
train	*kereta api*
plane	*pesawat terbang*

Directions

How do I get to …?	*Bagaimana saya pergi ke …?*
Is it far?	*Jauh?*
Is it near here?	*Dekat dari sini?*
Go straight ahead!	*Jalan terus!*
Turn left …	*Belok kiri …*
Turn right …	*Belok kanan …*
at the T-junction	*di pertigaan*
at the traffic lights	*di lampu lalu lintas*

in front of	*di depan*
next to	*di samping*
behind	*di belakang*
opposite	*berhadapan dengan*

north	*utara*
south	*selatan*
east	*timur*
west	*barat*

Air

For internal destinations, surface transportation is much cheaper, and in some cases more easily available, than flights. However you'll find that often the only alternative to a lengthy land or sea passage – particularly in the outer islands – is to take scheduled flights. There can be quite a difference in the fares offered by different agents for the same journey.

How much is a ... from Jakarta to Medan?	*Berapa harga satu ... dari Jakarta ke Medan?*
one-way ticket	*tiket satu jalan*
return ticket	*tiket pulang pergi*

Is there a flight to Medan on Monday?	*Apakah ada penerbangan ke Medan pada hari Senin?*
What time is the flight to Medan on Monday?	*Jam berapa penerbangan ke Medan pada hari Minggu?*
I would like to buy a return ticket.	*Saya akan beli satu tiket pulang pergi.*
What time do I have to be at the airport?	*Jam berapa saya harus tiba di lapangan terbang?*

Bus

The best way to travel long distances is to take an overnight express bus. These buses stop occasionally for meal and toilet stops and can only be boarded at city terminals. Day buses can be hailed or stopped anywhere along the road.

Booking Night Bus Tickets

Where can I buy a night bus ticket?	*Dimana saya bisa beli tiket bis malam?*
Is there any night bus to …?	*Apakah ada bis malam ke …?*
What time does the bus arrive at …?	*Jam berapa bis sampai di …?*
Will the bus stop at a restaurant?	*Apakah bis akan berhenti di restoran?*
I would like to book a seat for Monday.	*Saya akan pesan satu kursi untuk hari Senin.*

Travelling on a Day Bus

Two tickets to …	*Dua karcis ke …*
Does this bus go to …?	*Apakah bis ini pergi ke …?*
Which bus goes to …?	*Bis mana yang ke …?*
What time is the … bus?	*Jam berapa bis yang …?*
next	*berikutnya*
last	*terakhir*
Could you let me know when we arrive at …	*Tolong beritahu saya kalau sudah sampai di …*
I want to get off!	*Saya mau turun! (Kiri!)*

Train

Express trains require booked tickets whereas local train tickets can be bought just before departure.

Please give me two ... tickets.	*Minta dua karcis ...*
1st class	*kelas satu*
economy class	*kelas ekonomi*
I want to go by express train to ...	*Saya mau naik kereta ekspres ke ...*
Which platform does the train leave from?	*Dari peron berapa kereta berangkat?*
Where do I need to change trains?	*Dimana saya harus ganti kereta*
Is this seat free?	*Kursi ini kosong?*
This seat is taken.	*Sudah ada orangnya*
Would you mind if I open the window?	*Boleh saya buka jendela?*
What is this station called?	*Ini stasiun apa?*
What is the next station?	*Apa stasiun yang berikutnya?*

Taxi

There are official and unofficial taxis in Indonesia. Official taxis always have a sign but not necessarily a meter, whereas unofficial ones are privately owned cars used illegally as taxis. In taxis without meters, both official and unofficial, you will have to agree on a price before setting out.

Can you take me to …?	*Antar saya ke … ?*
this address	*alamat ini*
the airport	*lapangan terbang*

How much does it cost to go to …?	*Berapa ongkos ke … ?*
Does that include the luggage?	*Itu termasuk ongkos bagasi?*
That's too much!	*Terlalu mahal!*

Instructions

Here is fine, thank you.	*Berhenti disini.*
The next street, please.	*Jalan berikutnya.*
Continue!	*Terus!*
Please slow down.	*Pelan-pelan saja.*
Please hurry.	*Tolong cepat sedikit.*
Please wait here.	*Tunggu disini.*
I'll be right back.	*Saya akan kembali.*

Car

Where can I rent a car?	*Dimana saya bisa sewa mobil?*
How much is it daily/weekly?	*Berapa ongkos sewanya per hari/minggu?*
Does that include insurance?	*Apa itu termasuk asuransi?*
Where is the next petrol station?	*Dimana pompa bensin yang berikutnya?*
Is this the road to …?	*Apa ini jalan ke … ?*
I want … litres of petrol.	*Minta … liter bensin.*
Please fill up the tank.	*Tolong penuhi tangkinya.*

Problems

The battery is flat.	*Baterainya habis.*
The radiator is leaking.	*Radiatornya bocor.*
I have a flat tyre.	*Ban saya kempes.*
It is not working.	*Tidak bisa hidup.*

Useful Words

battery	*baterai*
brakes	*rem*
clutch	*kopeling*
engine	*mesin*
lights	*lampu*
tyres	*ban*
radiator	*radiator*
driver's licence	*SIM (Surat Ijin Mengemudi)*
No Entry	*dilarang masuk*
No Parking	*dilarang parkir*
One Way	*satu arah*

Local Transport

There's a great variety of local transport in Indonesia. This includes the ubiquitous Balinese *bemo* – a pick-up truck with two rows of seats down the sides or else a small minibus. Bemos usually run standard routes like buses and depart when full, but can also be chartered like a taxi. A step up from the bemo is the small minibus known either as an *oplet, microlet* or a *colt* – since they are often Mitsubishi Colts. In some towns bemos are now known as *angkots*, from *angkutan* (transport) and *kota* (city).

Then there's the *becak*, or bicycle-rickshaw – they're just the same as in so many other Asian countries, but are only found in towns and cities. Increasingly, they are being banned from the central areas of major cities. There are none in Bali. The *bajaj*, a three-wheeler powered by a noisy two-stroke engine, is only found in Jakarta. They're identical to what is known in India as an autorickshaw. In quieter towns, you may find *andongs* and *dokars* – horse or pony carts with two (dokars) or four (andongs) wheels.

Bargaining

How much does it cost to go to …?	*Berapa ongkos ke …?*
How about Rp 500?	*Bagaimana kalau Rp 500?*
Here is Rp1000.	*Ini uangnya Rp1000.*
How about my change?	*Mana kembalinya?*

Some Useful Phrases

The (train) is …	*(Kereta)nya …*
delayed	*ditunda*
cancelled	*dibatalkan*
on time	*tepat*

How long will it be delayed?	*Berapa lama ditundanya?*
Do I need to change trains?	*Apa saya harus ganti kereta?*
You must change …	*Anda harus ganti …*
How long does the trip take?	*Berapa lama perjalanan?*
I want to get off at …	*Saya mau turun di …*
I am lost.	*Saya tersesat.*
Where is the nearest bus station?	*Dimana setasiun bis yang terdekat?*
Where can I hire a bicycle?	*Dimana saya bisa sewa sepeda?*
Where do I get off to go to the International Bank?	*Dimana saya turun untuk pergi ke Bank Internasional?*
Where are we now?	*Dimana kita sekarang?*
Where is the restroom?	*Dimana kamar kecil?*

Some Useful Words

address	*alamat*
alley	*gang*
airport	*lapangan terbang*
station	*stasiun, terminal bis*
cabin	*ruang*
corner	*sudut*
confirmation	*penegasan*
dock	*dok*
early	*pagi-pagi*
economy class	*kelas ekonomi*
emergency	*darurat*
empty	*kosong*
fast	*cepat*
full	*penuh*
intersection	*persimpangan*
landing	*pendaratan*

late	*terlambat*
lounge	*kamar tunggu*
plane	*pesawat terbang*
port	*pelabuhan*
reservation	*pesanan tempat*
river	*sungai*
sail	*layar*
sea	*laut*
seat	*tempat duduk*
seat belt/safety belt	*sabuk*
station master	*kepala stasiun*
steward	*pramugara*
street	*jalan*
take off, depart	*berangkat*
timetable	*daftar waktu*
ticket	*karcis*
ticket window	*loket*
Danger!	*Berbahaya!*
Careful!	*Hati-hati!*
Wait!	*Tunggu!*
Stop!	*Stop!*

Accommodation

Indonesian hotels range in price and standard from the low to the high end of the market. Hotels of the Hilton and Hyatt style are found in the larger tourist areas. Cheaper and more interesting are the *losmen* – Indonesian hotels – which are also more abundant. The standard of these losmen ranges from very traditional, simple hotels with basic rooms (four walls and a couple of beds) and an outside bathroom *(mandi)*. These days most rooms in losmen have their own bathrooms. Many of these cheap hotels also have a few rooms with showers and air-conditioning available at additional cost. The great advantage of staying in losmen is that you'll meet Indonesian people travelling or on temporary work placements.

Finding Accommodation

Where is a …?	*Dimana ada …?*
hotel	*hotel*
losmen	*losmen*
nice hotel	*hotel bagus*
inexpensive hotel	*hotel murah*

I've already found a hotel.	*Saya sudah dapat hotel.*
Please take me to a hotel.	*Tolong antar saya ke hotel.*
What is the address?	*Di mana alamatnya?*
Could you write down the address, please?	*Tolong tulis alamatnya.*

At the Hotel
Checking In

I'd like a room ...	*Saya perlu satu kamar ...*
for one person	*untuk satu orang*
for two people	*untuk dua orang*
with a bathroom	*dengan kamar mandi*
with a TV	*dengan TV*
with a window	*dengan jendela*
I am going to stay for ...	*Saya mau tinggal ...*
one day	*satu hari*
one week	*satu minggu*
Is there a room available?	*Ada kamar kosong?*
How much does it cost per day?	*Berapa sewanya sehari?*
Does the price include breakfast?	*Apa sewanya termasuk makan pagi?*
Do you allow chidren?	*Boleh saya bawa anak?*
Is there extra cost for children?	*Ada sewa tambahan untuk anak?*
Can I see the room?	*Boleh saya lihat kamarnya?*
I don't like this room.	*Saya tidak suka kamar ini.*
Is there any better room?	*Ada kamar yang lebih bagus?*
I will take this room.	*Saya mau kamar ini.*

I'm not sure how long I'm staying.
Saya tidak tahu berapa lama saya akan tinggal disini.

Do I leave my key in reception?
Apakah saya perlu tinggal kunci kamar di resepsi?

During Your Stay

Where can I wash my clothes?
Dimana bisa mencuci baju?

Please wash these clothes for me.
Tolong cuci baju-baju ini.

When will they be ready?
Kapan bisa diambil?

Can I use the telephone?
Boleh pakai telpon?

Please spray my room. There are mosquitoes in it.
Tolong semprot kamar saya. Ada nyamuk.

Please change my sheets.
Tolong ganti sepreinya.

My room needs to be cleaned.
Tolong bersihkan kamar saya.

Complaints

Excuse me, I've got a problem here.
Maaf, ada masalah disini.

I can't open the door/window.
Pintunya/jendelanya tidak bisa dibuka.

I've locked myself out.
Kunci saya tertinggal di kamar.

The toilet won't flush.
WCnya tidak bisa disiram.

Can you get it fixed?
Bisa diperbaiki?

The room smells.
Kamarnya bau.

It's too dark.
Terlalu gelap disini.

It's too noisy.
Terlalu bising disini.

Checking Out

I am leaving this hotel.	*Saya akan meninggalkan hotel ini.*
Please prepare our bill.	*Tolong siapkan rekening saya.*
Call me a taxi please.	*Tolong panggilkan taksi.*

Can I pay by ...?	*Bisa bayar dengan ...?*
credit card	*kartu kredit*
traveller's cheque	*cek wisata*

Can I leave my things here until ...?	*Bisa titip barang sampai ...?*
this afternoon	*nanti siang*
this evening	*nanti sore*

Some Useful Phrases

The hotel is near (the) ...	*Hotelnya dekat ...*
street	*jalan*
alley	*gang*
beach	*pantai*
shop	*toko*

I want to have ...	*Saya mau ...*
breakfast	*makan pagi*
lunch	*makan siang*
dinner	*makan malam*

I want to drink ...	*Saya mau minum ...*
tea	*teh*
coffee	*kopi*

boiled water	*air rebus*
cold water	*air dingin*

Some Useful Words

address	*alamat*
air-conditioner	*AC*
	(pronounced: 'ah-chay')
bathe (v)	*mandi*
blanket	*selimut*
candle	*lilin*
chair	*kursi*
clean (adj)	*bersih*
crowded	*ramai*
cupboard	*lemari*
dark	*gelap*
dirty	*kotor*
door	*pintu*
dust (n)	*debu*
eat (v)	*makan*
electricity	*listrik*
garden	*kebun*
hedge	*pagar*
key, lock	*kunci*
lift	*lift*
mattress	*kasur*
mirror	*cermin*
pillow	*bantal*
noisy	*ramai*
quiet	*sepi*
rent (v)	*menyewa*
roof	*atap*

servant	*pembantu*
sit (v)	*duduk*
sheet	*seprei*
sleep (v)	*tidur*
soap	*sabun mandi*
swimming pool	*kolam renang*
table	*meja*
towel	*handuk*
wake (v)	*bangun*
wash (v)	*cuci*
water	*air*

Around Town

Where is a ...	Dimana ada ...
bank	*bank*
barber	*tukang cukur*
barong dance	*tari barong*
bookshop	*toko buku*
cinema	*bioskop*
concert	*konser*
consulate	*konsulat*
crossroad	*perempatan*
embassy	*kedutaan besar*
garden	*kebun*
hospital	*rumah sakit*
hotel	*hotel*
market	*pasar*
museum	*musium*
park	*taman*
police station	*kantor polisi*
post office	*kantor pos*
public telephone	*telepon umum*
public toilet	*WC umum*
puppet theatre	*wayang kulit*
restaurant	*rumah makan*
school	*sekolah*
temple	*candi*
theatre	*gedung sandiwara*
town square	*alun-alun*
village	*desa*
zoo	*kebun binatang*

How far is the …?	*Berapa jauh …?*
I am going to the …	*Saya mau pergi ke …*
I want to see the …	*Saya mau lihat …*
I am looking for the …	*Saya mencari …*
What time does it open?	*Jam berapa buka?*
What time does it close?	*Jam berapa tutup?*
Is it still open?	*Masih buka?*

What … is this?	*Ini … apa?*
street	*jalan*
city	*kota*

At the Post Office

I want to buy …	*Saya mau beli …*
postcards	*kartu pos*
stamps	*perangko*

I want to send a …	*Saya mau kirim …*
letter	*surat*
parcel	*paket*
telegram	*kawat*

Please send it …	*Tolong kirim dengan …*
airmail	*pos udara*
surface mail	*pos biasa*
express (overseas)	*ekspres*
express (internal)	*kilat*

Some Useful Phrases

How much is an airmail letter to the USA?	*Berapa perankonya kirim surat dengan pos udara ke Amerika?*

Please send this parcel to England by surface mail.	*Kirimkan paket ini ke England dengan pos biasa.*
Please weigh this letter.	*Tolong timbang berat surat ini.*
Please stamp this letter immediately.	*Tolong tempelkan surat ini sekarang.*
How much does it cost to send this to ...?	*Berapa ongkos kirim ini ke ...?*

Some Useful Words

aerogram	*aerogram*
envelope	*amplop*
mailbox	*bis surat*
postage	*bea*
receiver (letter)	*penerima*
sender (letter)	*pengirim*

Telephone

I want to call ...	*Saya mau menelpon ...*
The number is ...	*Nomernya ...*
I want to speak for three minutes.	*Saya mau bicara tiga menit.*
How much does a three-minute call cost?	*Berapa ongkos tiga menit telpon?*
I want to make a long-distance call to Australia.	*Saya mau menelpon ke Australia.*
I want to make a reverse-charges phone call.	*Saya mau menelpon yang dibayar oleh si penerima.*
Operator, I've been cut off.	*Operator, teleponnya terputus.*
The line is busy.	*Teleponnya sedang bicara.*

I would like to speak to …	*Saya mau bicara dengan …*
Sorry, you have the wrong number.	*Maaf, anda salah nomor.*
Hello, do you speak English?	*Halo, anda bisa bahasa Inggris?*
Hello, is … there?	*Halo, … ada?*
Yes, he/she is here.	*Ya, dia ada.*
One moment, please.	*Tunggu sebentar.*

At the Bank

I want to change …	*Saya mau menukar …*
US dollars	*dolar Amerika*
Australian dollars	*dolar Australi*
bank draft	*surat wesel*
cash	*uang kontan*
cheque	*cek*
letter of credit	*surat kredit*
money	*uang*
travellers' cheque	*cek turis*

Some Useful Phrases

What time does the bank open?	*Jam berapa bank buka?*
Where can I cash a travellers' cheque?	*Dimana saya bisa menguangkan cek perjalanan turis?*
What is the exchange rate?	*Berapa perbandingan harga?*
Has any money arrived for me?	*Ada kiriman uang untuk saya?*
Can I transfer money here from my bank?	*Bisakah mentransfer uang dari bank saya ke sini?*

| How long will it take to arrive? | *Berapa lama waktu yang diperlukan?* |

Some Useful Words

bank clerk	*pegawai bank*
bill, note	*uang kertas*
branch	*cabang*
coins	*uang logam*
commission	*komisi*
endorsement	*pengesyahan*
ID card	*K.T.P.*
signature	*tanda tangan*
teller	*kasir*
ticket window	*loket*

Sightseeing

Where is the tourist office?	*Dimana ada kantor wisata?*
What is that building?	*Itu gedung apa?*
What is this monument?	*Ini monumen apa?*
Who lived there?	*Siapa yang tinggal di sana dulu?*
Do you have a local map?	*Anda punya peta lokal?*
Can I take photographs?	*Boleh saya foto?*
Can I take your photograph?	*Boleh saya foto anda?*
I will send you the photograph.	*Saya akan kirim fotonya.*
Could you take a photograph of me?	*Tolong foto say.*
At what theatre can I see a play?	*Di teater mana boleh saya menonton sandiwara?*

| How did you enjoy the play? | *Sukakah anda pada sandiwara itu?* |
| I am interested in music. | *Saya suka musik.* |

Some Useful Words

castle	*benteng*
church	*gereja*
crowded	*ramai*
empty	*kosong*
interesting	*menarik hati*
mosque	*mesjid*
nice	*bagus*
statue	*patung*
ticket	*karcis*
university	*universitas*
nightclub	*kelab malam*

Bureaucracy

If you need to have dealings with the Indonesian bureaucracy for any reason, there are a couple of things you ought to remember. Always dress decently. Try to speak to the person in charge – you will get more information this way and there is a good chance they will speak some English. With their English and your Indonesian you shouldn't have too many problems. In descending order of importance the official titles are:

head of province	*bupati*
head of a district	*camat*
head of an area	*kepala desa*
village chief	*kepala kampung*

Forms

name	*nama*
address	*alamat*
date of birth	*tanggal lahir*
place of birth	*tempat lahir*
age	*umur*
sex	*jenis kelamin*
nationality	*kebangsaan*
religion	*agama*
profession	*pekerjaan*
reason for travel	*maksud kunjungan*
marital status	*kawin*
identification	*surat keterangan*
passport number	*nomor paspor*
visa	*visa*
birth certificate	*surat keterangan lahir*
driver's licence	*S.I.M. (Surat Ijin Mengemudi)*
customs	*bea cukai*
immigration	*imigrasi*

In the Country

When you go camping or hiking in Indonesia, you will discover that most directions are given in terms of compass points – left and right are not used very often. The compass points are:

north	*utara*
south	*selatan*
east	*timur*
west	*barat*

Indonesians are very polite people and like to be agreeable. If you simply ask 'Is this north?', they may just agree with you, so it's preferable to use *Dimana utara?*, Where is north?, to get your bearings. If there is any doubt, ask several different people. Remember that in Bali 'north' traditionally means 'towards the mountains'.

Weather

What's the weather like?	*Bagaimana cuacanya?*

Today it is ...	*Hari ini ...*
cloudy	*mendung*
cold	*dingin*
raining heavily	*hujan lebat*
raining lightly	*gerimis*
warm	*hangat*
wet	*basah*
windy	*berangin*

hot	*panas*
humid	*lembab*

What time is …?	*Jam berapa …?*
sunrise	*matahari terbit*
sunset	*matahari terbenam*

Some Useful Words

cloud	*awan*
dry season	*musim kemarau*
earth	*bumi*
fog	*kabut*
mud	*lumpur*
rain	*hujan*

rainy season	*musim hujan*
smoke	*asap*
storm	*badai*
sun	*mata hari*
	(literally: eye of the day)

Geographical Terms

beach	*pantai*
bridge	*jembatan*
cave	*gua*
city	*kota*
estuary	*kuala*
forest	*hutan*
harbour	*pelabuan*
hill	*bukit*
hot spring	*mata air panas*
island	*pulau*
lake	*danau*
mountain	*gunung*
plain	*dataran*
river	*sungai*
sea	*laut*
valley	*lembah*
village	*desa*
waterfall	*air terjun*

Plants & Agriculture

agriculture	*pertanian*
cloves	*cengkeh*
coconut palm	*pohon kelapa*
corn	*jagung*

firewood	*kayu bakar*
flower	*bunga*
fruit tree	*pohon buah*
harvest (v)	*panen*
irrigation	*pengairan*
leaf	*daun*
planting	*menanam*
rice field	*sawah*
rice terrace	*petak sawah*
sugar cane	*tebu*
tobacco	*tembakau*

Animals & Birds

bird	*burung*
buffalo	*kerbau*
cat	*kucing*
chicken	*ayam*
cow	*sapi*
crocodile	*buaya*
dog	*anjing*
fish	*ikan*
frog	*katak*
goat	*kambing*
horse	*kuda*
leech	*lintah*
lion	*singa*
monkey	*monyet*
pig	*babi*
rooster	*ayam jantan*
sheep	*domba*
snake	*ular*

spider	*laba-laba*
tiger	*harimau*

Insects

ant	*semut*
butterfly	*kupu-kupu*
cockroach	*kecoa*
fly	*lalat*
mosquito	*nyamuk*

Outdoor Activities

mountain climbing	*naik gunung*
diving	*selam*
fishing	*memancing*
hunting	*berburuh*
surfing	*bermain selancar*
swimming	*berenang*

Some Useful Words

backpack	*ransel*
campground	*tempat kemah*
camping	*kemah*
compass	*kompas*
mat	*tikar*
penknife	*pisau lipat*
rope	*tali*
stove	*kompor*
tent	*tenda*
torch (flashlight)	*senter*

Some Useful Phrases

Are there any tourist attractions near here?	*Ada tempat pariwisata disini?*
Is it safe to swim here?	*Aman berenang disini?*
There are two caves here.	*Ada dua gua disini.*
Where is the nearest village?	*Di mana desa yang paling dekat?*
Is it safe to climb this mountain?	*Aman naik gunung itu?*

| Is there a hut up there? | *Ada pondok di atas?* |
| Do I need a guide? | *Apakah saya perlu pemandu wisata?* |

Food

The simplicity of Indonesian is very easy to see when it comes to words connected with food and eating. *Makan* is both the verb 'to eat' and a general word concerning food. A restaurant is an 'eating house', *rumah makan*. Breakfast is 'morning food', *makan pagi*. In addition you will find that eating out in Indonesia is a very informal affair. There are basically three options: hotel restaurants where the food is expensive but not necessarily the best; *warung*, the temporary food stalls which are set up every evening and which serve the best genuine local delicacies at low prices; and the intermediate option, which is to visit one of the host of local restaurants which line the main street of any town.

Where is a ...	*Dimana ada ...*
cheap restaurant	*rumah makan murah*
restaurant	*rumah makan*
food stall	*warung*
night market	*pasar malam*

At the Restaurant

We would like a table for five, please.	*Minta meja untuk lima orang.*

Please bring ...	*Bolehkah saya minta ...*
the menu	*daftar makanan*
a glass of water	*segelas air putih*
the bill	*bon*

I can't eat …	*Saya tidak makan …*
milk and cheese	*susu dan keju*
eggs	*telur*
meat	*daging*
prawns	*udang*

This isn't cooked.	*Belum masak.*
Not too spicy please.	*Jangan terlalu pedas.*
No MSG please.	*Jangan pakai Aji-ni-moto/*
	bumbu masak.
This is delicious.	*Makanan ini enak.*

At the Market

The market is the dynamic focal point of life in any Indonesian town. In the market the most intriguing array of local produce will be laid out for sale, including all the locally grown fruits. Although the greatest range of fruits is available in the wet season, there is always some fresh fruit on offer.

There are always bananas, *pisang*, which are found in a multitude of forms, and are about the cheapest fruit. Rambutans, *rambutan*, are a bright red fruit covered in soft, hairy spines, containing a delicious, lychee-like, sweet white flesh. The mangosteen, *manggis*, is very sought after for its mouth-watering sweet-sour white flesh, and is easily recognised by its thick purple-brown fibrous outer covering which protects the segmented fruit inside.

Don't let the perfect brown 'snakeskin' covering deter you from buying and trying a few *salak*. They are the fruit of the Zalacca palm and the flesh is crunchy and nutty in flavour. Jackfruit (*nangka*) trees are widely grown in homegardens, and can be recognised by huge pendulous fruit, often wrapped in a large plastic bag for protection while they ripen on the tree. Jackfruit sellers often break the whole fruit up into individual segments, which are then packed, ready to eat, into small plastic bags for sale in the market. The flesh is rubbery and sweet, and rather strongly flavoured.

An encounter with a durian, *durian*, the 'king of fruits', is a most memorable experience for the fruit lover. Durians announce themselves in any market by exuding an incredibly pungent

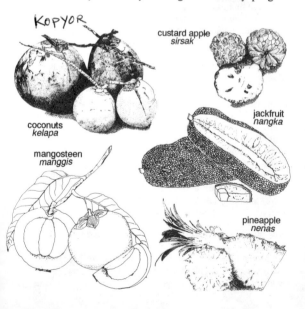

KOPYOR

coconuts
kelapa

custard apple
sirsak

jackfruit
nangka

mangosteen
manggis

pineapple
nenas

stench. If you can hold your breath long enough to approach, and swallow the rich, creamy flesh, you will get to appreciate an absolutely unique flavour.

Starfruit, *belimbing*, is a watery thirst-quenching fruit, shaped like a star when viewed end on. It is one of the few fruits which are eaten without being peeled or having their outer covering removed. A good wash in clean water is advisable.

Most tropical fruits are soft, even mushy, so it's a refreshing change to find a crunchy, almost woody textured fruit, such as the guava or *jambu*. It is a hard, pear-shaped fruit, with small black seeds which should not be eaten.

There are other more familiar fruits available as well. Mangoes, *mangga*, when in season are delicious; pineapples, *nanas*, are invariably extremely sweet, and lacking the acid bite we often associate with pineapples grown in temperate climates; while coconuts, *kelapa*, are very familiar to most Indonesians. The young coconut, *kelapa muda*, lopped off the nearest coconut palm makes a delightfully refreshing, naturally sterile drink. Pawpaws, *papaya*, are ubiquitous and can be found in a number of different varieties.

An unusual fruit salad made from the unripe flesh of the pawpaw, mango, jambu or starfruit is a favourite of the Javanese. It is sweetened with palm sugar and flavoured with ground chillies. Green fruit and fresh chillies present a challenge to a weak stomach – take care!

How much is a kg of …?	*Sekilo … berapa?*
A kg of …, please.	*Sekilo …*
I don't want that one.	*Jangan yang itu.*
Please give me that other one.	*Yang lainya.*

Meals

breakfast	*makan pagi*
lunch	*makan siang*
dinner	*makan malam*

Meat — Daging

beef	*daging sapi*
brains	*otak*
chicken	*ayam*
duck	*daging bebek*
heart	*jantung*
lamb	*domba*
liver	*hati*
mutton, goat	*kambing*

Fruit & Nuts — Buah & Kacang

apples	*apel*
banana	*pisang*
coconut	*kelapa*
durian	*durian*
jackfruit	*nangka*
lemon	*jeruk asam*
mangosteen	*manggis*
mango	*mangga*
orange	*jeruk manis*
pawpaw	*papaya*
peanuts	*kacang*
pineapple	*nanas*
starfruit	*belimbing*
strawberry	*arbei*

Vegetables   *Sayur*

Most vegetables are simply called *sayur*, without having an individual name. If you are a vegetarian you can say *tanpa daging*, without meat, or *sayur saja*, vegetables only.

beans	*buncis*
cabbage	*kol*
carrot	*wartol*
cauliflower	*bunga kol*
corn	*jagung*
cucumber	*mentimun*
eggplant	*terung*
mushrooms	*jamur*
onion	*bawang bombay*
potato	*kentang*
pumpkin	*labu merah*
tomato	*tomat*

Staples

bread	*roti tawar*
noodles	*mie*
rice	*nasi*

Snacks

biscuits	*biskit*
boiled egg	*telur rebus*
cake	*kue*
egg	*telur*
sweets	*manisan*

Spices & Condiments

chilli	*cabe*
cinnamon	*kayu manis*
cloves	*cengkeh*
curry	*kari*
garlic	*bawang putih*
ginger	*jahe*
oil	*minyak*
pepper	*lada*
salt	*garam*
soy sauce	*kecap asin*
sweet soy sauce	*kecap manis*
sugar	*gula*
turmeric	*kunyit*
vinegar	*cuka*

Seafood — *Ikan*

crab	*kepiting*
freshwater fish	*ikan tambak*
lobster	*udang karang*
oysters	*tiram*
saltwater fish	*ikan laut*
shrimp	*udang*

Drinks
Cold Drinks

beer	*bir*
boiled water	*air putih*
chocolate	*coklat*
citrus juice	*es jeruk*
coconut milk	*es kelapa*

cordial	*es sirup*
ginger tea	*jahe*
milk	*susu*
rice wine	*brem*

Hot Drinks

coffee	*kopi*
tea	*teh*
with/without milk	*dengan/tanpa susu*
with/without sugar	*dengan/tanpa gula*

Cooking Methods

baked	*panggang*
boiled	*rebus*
fried	*goreng*
grilled	*bakar*
steamed	*kukus*
smoked	*asap*

Special Dishes

Every region of Indonesia has its own special dishes, which you will want to try out. The best place to find the local dishes is at the food stalls along the street, because that's where the local people eat. Just go along and see what is being served.

chicken soup	*sop ayam*
cold vegetable salad with peanut sauce	*gado-gado*
meat grilled on skewers	*sate*
mixed vegetables (Chinese dish)	*cap cai*

noodle soup	*mie kuah*
pancake with accompaniments	*martabak*
rice	*nasi*
boiled rice	*nasi putih*
fried rice	*nasi goreng*
rice and vegetables	*nasi sayur*
rice with a selection of things, including meat	*nasi campur*
roast piglet	*babi guling*

Some Useful Words

ashtray	*asbak*
bitter	*pahit*
boil (v)	*merebus*
boiled	*rebus*
cold	*dingin*
cook (v)	*masak*
delicious	*enak*
eat (v)	*makan*
foreign	*asing*
fresh	*segar*
fry (v)	*goreng*
good	*bagus*
hot	*panas*
indigenous	*asli*
salty	*asin*
slice (v)	*iris*
sour	*asam*
spicy	*pedas*
sweet	*manis*

toothpick   *tusuk gigi*
unripe/uncooked   *mentah*

Some Useful Phrases

Can we have breakfast at this food stall?   *Bagaimana jika kita makan pagi di warung ini?*

I'm sorry but this table is reserved.   *Maaf, meja ini sudah dipesan.*

We're in a hurry. Please bring our orders quickly.   *Kami terburu-buru. Tolong makanan kami, cepat.*

May we have our bill please?   *Minta bonnya.*

Shopping

In Indonesia it is customary to bargain, but this is mainly in the market or for services like taxis and pedicabs. In shops and restaurants, or wherever prices are marked on the items, bargaining is not customary. This is known as fixed price or *harga pas*. It is quite common for tourists to be charged more than the local people, as they are often considered to be wealthy. Even so, tourists do not usually pay a great deal more than the locals and if you want to know the common price, *harga biasa*, ask an independent bystander. On the public transport system watch what everybody else is paying. For long trips, or boat trips, expect to pay a little more than the locals. Bargaining is part of the way of life in Indonesia. If you treat it like a game it can be fun, even worthwhile, but remember that the 500 rupiah price difference you may be getting so upset about is really only a few cents to you.

Where is the ...?	*Dimana ada ... ?*
barber	*tukang cukur*
bookshop	*toko buku*
chemist	*apotik*
drug store	*toko obat*
market	*pasar*
night market	*pasar malam*
shopping centre	*pusat pertokoan*
tailor	*penjahit*

I want to buy ...	*Saya mau beli ...*
that basket	*keranjang itu*
that bottle	*botol itu*

buttons	*kancing*
combs	*sisir*
jar	*toples*
mosquito net	*kelambu*
rope	*tambang*
sarong material	*kain sarong*
suitcase	*kopor*
thread	*benang*
torch (flashlight)	*obor*
towel	*handuk*

Bargaining

That's very expensive.	*Mahal sekali.*
I don't have much money.	*Saya tidak ada banyak uang.*
Can you lower the price?	*Boleh kurang?*
I'll give you ...	*Saya bayar ...*
No more than ...	*Tidak lebih dari ...*

Souvenirs

bone	*tulang*
earrings	*anting-anting*
gold	*mas*
handicraft	*kerajinan tangan*
handmade batik	*batik tulis*
horn	*tanduk*
ivory	*gading*
jewellery	*intan permata*
leather	*kulit*
masks	*topeng*
material	*kain*
necklace	*kalung*

paintings	*lukisan*
pottery	*keramik*
printed batik	*batik cap*
puppets	*wayang kulit*
ring	*cincin*
silver	*perak*
souvenir	*kenang-kenangan*
stone carvings	*ukiran batu*
woodcarving	*ukiran kayu*

Clothing

bras	*beha*
clothing	*pakaian*
dress	*rok*
gloves	*sarung tangan*
hat	*topi*
jacket	*jaket*
jeans	*jean*
jumper	*jamper*
sandals	*sandal*
shirt	*kemeja*
shorts	*celana pendek*
shoes	*sepatu*
socks	*kaos kaki*
swimsuit	*baju renang*
tie	*dasi*
trousers	*celana panjang*
T-shirt	*kaos*
underwear	*celana dalam*

Materials

cotton	*katun*
leather	*kulit*
silk	*sutera*
wool	*wol*

Colours

black	*hitam*
blue	*biru*
brown	*coklat*
colour	*warna*

dark	*tua*
green	*hijau*
light	*muda*
orange	*jingga*
pink	*merah muda*
purple	*ungu*
red	*merah*
white	*putih*
yellow	*kuning*

Toiletries

baby's bottle	*botol bayi*
baby powder	*bedak bayi*
condoms	*kondom*
contraceptive	*kontrasepsi*
laxative	*obat cuci perut*
moisturising cream	*krim pelembab*
mosquito repellent	*obat nyamuk*
razor	*alat cukur*
sanitary napkins	*softex*

shampoo	*sampo*
shaving cream	*sabun cukur*
sunblock cream	*krim pencegah kulit terbakar sinar matahari*
tampons	*tampon*
tissues	*tisu*
toilet paper	*kertas kamar kecil*
toothbrush	*sikat gigi*
toothpaste	*odol*

Stationery & Publications

ballpoint pen	*pena bolpoin*
a bilingual dictionary	*kamus dua bahasa*
envelopes	*amplop*
a magazine	*majalah*
map	*peta*
the morning newspaper	*koran pagi*
English newspaper	*koran bahasa Inggris*
novel	*novel*
a pocket dictionary	*kamus saku*
scissors	*gunting*
writing paper	*kertas tulis*

Photography

I'd like a film for this camera.	*Minta filem untuk kamera ini.*
How much is it for processing and developing?	*Berapa ongkos cuci cetak?*
When will it be ready?	*Kapan selesai?*
Do you repair cameras?	*Bisa memperbaiki kamera disini?*

B&W (film)	*hitam/putih*
camera	*kamera*
colour (film)	*warna*
to develop	*mencuci*
film	*filem*
photograph	*foto*

Smoking

cigarettes	*rokok*
matches	*korek api*
pipe	*pipa rokok*
tobacco	*tembakau*
A packet of cigarettes, please	*Minta satu bungkus rokok.*
Do you have a light?	*Minta api?*

Weights & Measures

gm	*gram*
kg	*kg*
mm	*milimeter*
cm	*sentimeter*
metre	*meter*
km	*kilometer*
litre	*liter*

Sizes & Comparisons

big	*besar*
bigger	*lebih besar*
biggest	*paling besar*
too big	*terlalu besar*
small	*kecil*

smaller	*lebih kecil*
smallest	*paling kecil*
enough	*cukup*
less	*kurang*
more	*lebih banyak*
heavy	*berat*
light	*ringan*
long	*panjang*
short	*pendek*
tall	*tinggi*

Some Useful Words

buy (v)	*beli*
cheap	*murah*
discount	*korting*
expensive	*mahal*
export (v)	*mengekspor*
import (v)	*mengimpor*
like (v)	*suka*
made in	*dibuat di*
old	*tua*
order (v)	*pesan*
parcel	*bungkus*
prefer	*lebih suka*
quality	*kwalitas*
quantity	*jumlah*
round	*bulat*
sell	*jual*
small	*kecil*
style	*macam*
want (v)	*mau*

Some Useful Phrases

I'm just looking.	*Saya hanya lihat-lihat.*
What is the normal price of this?	*Berapa harga biasa itu?*
Can you write down the price?	*Tolong tulis harganya.*
Do you accept credit cards?	*Bisa bayar dengan kartu kredit?*
May I try this on?	*Boleh saya coba?*
Do you have others?	*Ada yang lain?*
We don't have any.	*Tidak ada lagi.*
Can I see it?	*Boleh saya lihat?*
I don't like it.	*Saya tidak suka ini.*
I will take it.	*Saya beli ini.*
I'd like to look at blouses.	*Saya ingin melihat-lihat blus.*
How much is this?	*Berapa harga ini?*
Where are these goods made?	*Barang-barang ini dibuatdimana?*
Do I need insurance?	*Apakah saya perlu asuransi?*
free of charge	*gratis*

Health

With luck your time in Indonesia will be without illness and you will not need to turn to this section at all.

Sakit is an all-purpose word about illness. As a verb *sakit* means 'to feel sick' or 'to hurt', as an adjective it means 'sick' or 'painful'. For example: the hospital, *rumah sakit;* I feel ill, *Saya sakit.*

Where is a ...   *Dimana ada ...*
    dentist   *doktergigi*
    doctor   *dokter*
    drug store   *toko obat*
    hospital   *rumah sakit*
    medicine   *obat*
    pharmacy   *apotik*

At the Doctor

I'm suffering from ...	*Saya sakit ...*
I am allergic to ...	*Saya alergi ...*
My ... hurts	*... saya sakit.*
I feel nauseous.	*Saya mau muntah.*
I keep vomiting.	*Saya muntah terus.*
I feel dizzy.	*Saya pusing.*
I'm allergic to penicillin/ antibiotics.	*Saya alergi penisilin/antibiotika.*
I have low/high blood pressure.	*Saya menderita tekanan darah rendah/tinggi.*

Could I see a female doctor?	*Ada dokter yang perempuan disini?*
I'm pregnant.	*Saya hamil.*
I'm on the pill.	*Saya pakai pil kontrasepsi.*
I haven't menstruated for ... weeks.	*Saya tidak mentruasi selama ... minggu.*
I've been vaccinated.	*Saya sudah divaksinasi.*
I have my own syringe.	*Saya punya suntikan.*
I've had a blood test.	*Darah saya sudah diperiksa.*
I need a blood test.	*Saya perlu periksa darah.*
Please use this syringe.	*Pakai suntikan ini.*
How many times a day?	*Berapa kali sehari?*

Ailments

allergy	*alergi*
asthma	*asma*
burns	*luka bakar*
cholera	*kolera*
cold	*masuk angin*
constipation	*sembelit*
cough (v)	*batuk*
diarrhoea	*diare*
dysentery	*disenteri*
fever	*demam*
flu	*selesma*
food poisoning	*salah makan*
headache	*sakit kepala*
hepatitis	*hepatitis*
high blood pressure	*darah tinggi*
infection	*infeksi*
itch	*gatal*

lice	*kutu*
malaria	*malaria*
pain	*sakit*
rabies	*rabies*
rheumatism	*encok*
sore throat	*tenggorokan*
stomachache	*sakit perut*
sunburn	*kulit terbakar*
typhoid	*demam tipus*
venereal disease	*penyakit kelamin*
worms	*cacingan*
wound	*luka*

Parts of the Body

arm	*lengan*
back	*punggung*
bone	*tulang*
breast	*buah dada*
chest	*dada*
ear	*telinga*
eye	*mata*
face	*wajah*
finger	*jari tangan*
hands	*tangan*
head	*kepala*
heart	*jantung*
kidney	*ginjal*
leg/foot	*kaki*
liver	*hati*
lung	*paru-paru*
mouth	*mulut*

muscle	*otot*
neck	*leher*
nose	*hidung*
shoulder	*bahu*
skin	*kulit*
stomach	*perut*
tooth	*gigi*

Medicine

| antibiotics | *antibiotis* |
| antiseptic | *antiseptik* |

aspirin	*aspirin*
penicillin	*penisilin*
quinine	*kina*
sleeping pills	*pil tidur*
tablet	*tablet*
vitamins	*vitamin*

Some Useful Words

accident	*kecelakaan*
addiction	*kecanduan*
allergic	*alergi*
bandage	*pembalut*
bleed (v)	*berdarah*
blood	*darah*
broken	*patah*
breath	*nafas*
burn (v)	*bakar*
careful	*hati-hati*
collapse (v)	*ambruk*
compress	*kompres*
contraceptive	*kontrasepsi*
dog bite	*digigit anjing*
disease	*penyakit*
faeces	*berak*
fast (v, n)	*puasa*
health	*kesehatan*
injection	*suntikan*
menstruation	*menstruasi*
oxygen	*oksigen*
poisonous	*beracun*
prescription	*resep*

| urine | *air seni* |
| vomit (v) | *muntah* |

At the Chemist

I need medicine for …	*Saya perlu obat untuk …*
I need a prescription for …	*Apakah saya perlu resep untuk …*
These tablets must be taken three times a day.	*Tablet-tablet ini harus diminum tiga kali sehari.*
Please shake the bottle before taking.	*Kocok dulu sebelum diminum.*

At the Dentist

My tooth hurts.	*Gigi saya sakit.*
I've lost a filling.	*Tambalan gigi saya hilang.*
I've broken a tooth.	*Gigi saya patah.*
My gums hurt.	*Gusi saya sakit.*
I don't want it extracted.	*Jangan dicabut.*
Please give me an anaesthetic.	*Tolong beri saya obat matirasa.*

Some Useful Phrases

Please take us to a hospital.	*Antar kami ke rumah sakit.*
Please buy medicine for me at the pharmacy.	*Tolong beli obat untuk saya di apotik.*
My leg is broken.	*Kaki saya patah.*
I need a receipt for my insurance.	*Saya perlu kwitansi untuk asuransi saya.*

Time & Dates

Telling the Time

Telling the time in Indonesia is fairly straightforward. The English 'am' and 'pm' are replaced by whole words rather than abbreviations. For example, '8 am' is literally *delapan pagi*, '8 in the morning'; '8 pm' is *delapan malam*, '8 at night'.

hour	*jam*
minute	*menit*
second	*detik*
plus (past)	*lewat*
minus (to)	*kurang*
half	*setengah*

What time is it?	*Jam berapa?*
It is three o'clock.	*Jam tiga.*
It is a quarter to four.	*Jam empat kurang seperempat.*
It is a quarter past four.	*Jam empat lewat seperempat*
It is ten past three.	*Jam tiga lewat sepuluh.*
It is ten to four.	*Jam empat kurang sepuluh.*
It is rubber time.	*Jam karet.* (always gets a laugh)
It is five-thirty.	*Jam setengah enam.*

Unlike English, five thirty is not given in Indonesian as half past five but as half to six.

o'clock	*jam*
in the morning (1 – 11 am)	*pagi*

in the afternoon (11 am – 3 pm)	*siang*
in the evening (3 – 6 pm)	*sore*
at night (6 – 12 pm)	*malam*

Days of the Week

Monday	*hari Senin*
Tuesday	*hari Selasa*
Wednesday	*hari Rabu*
Thursday	*hari Kamis*
Friday	*hari Jumat*
Saturday	*hari Sabtu*
Sunday	*hari Minggu*

Months

January	*Januari*
February	*Februari*
March	*Maret*
April	*April*
May	*Mei*
June	*Juni*
July	*Juli*
August	*Agustus*
September	*September*
October	*Oktober*
November	*Nopember*
December	*Desember*

Dates

The number of the day precedes the name of the month in Indonesian dates.

17 August 1945
  (Independence Day)
	*tujuhbelas Agustus
	    sembilanbelas empatpuluh
	    lima*

Some Useful Phrases

What date is it today?	*Tanggal berapa hari ini?*
It's 28 June.	*Tanggal duapuluh delapan Juni.*
It's 1 April.	*Tanggal satu April.*

When did you come to Indonesia?	*Kapan tiba di Indonesia?*
Two weeks ago.	*Dua minggu yang lalu.*
How long will you stay?	*Berapa lama anda akan tinggal?*
I'll be staying (another) two weeks.	*Saya akan tinggal dua minggu lagi.*

Present

today	*hari ini*
this morning	*pagi ini*
this afternoon	*siang ini*
tonight	*malam ini*
this week	*minggu ini*
this month	*bulan ini*
this year	*tahun ini*
now	*sekarang*
immediately	*sekarang juga*
just now	*baru saja*

Past

yesterday	*kemarin*
day before yesterday	*kemarin dulu*
yesterday morning	*kemarin pagi*
yesterday aftrenoon	*kemarin siang*
last night	*kemarin malam*
last week	*minggu lalu*
last month	*bulan lalu*
last year	*tahun lalu*
ago	*yang lalu*
already	*sudah*

Future

tomorrow	*besok*
tomorrow morning	*besok pagi*
tomorrow evening	*besok sore*
day after tomorrow	*lusa*
next week	*minggu depan*
next month	*bulan depan*
next year	*tahun depan*
later	*nanti*
after	*sesudah*
not yet	*belum*

During the Day

sunrise	*matahari terbit*
dawn	*pagi buta*
sunset	*matahari terbenam*
midnight	*tengah malam*

Some Useful Words

a while ago	*beberapa waktu yang lalu*
a moment	*sebentar*
after	*sesudah*
always	*selalu*
before	*sebelum*
century	*abad*
day	*hari*
early	*awal*
everyday	*setiap hari*
forever	*selamanya*
fortnight	*dua minggu*
long ago	*dulu*

month	*bulan*
never	*tidak pernah*
not any more	*tidak lagi*
not yet	*belum*
recently	*baru-baru ini*
sometimes	*kadang-kadang*
soon	*segera*
week	*minggu*
year	*tahun*

Numbers & Amounts

Indonesian numbers are quite straightforward. Numbers from 11 to 19 are comprised of the numbers one to nine plus the suffix *belas*. Numbers after that are counted with the suffix of 10 – *puluh*. *Sepuluh* is 10, *duapuluh* is 20 and so on until the hundreds, when the suffix *ratus* is used. So *seratus* is 100, *duaratus* is 200, and so on. *Ribu* is the suffix for a thousand.

Cardinal Numbers

0	*nol*	19	*sembilanbelas*
1	*satu*	20	*duapuluh*
2	*dua*	21	*duapuluh satu*
3	*tiga*	22	*duapuluh dua*
4	*empat*	30	*tigapuluh*
5	*lima*	40	*empatpuluh*
6	*enam*	50	*limapuluh*
7	*tujuh*	100	*seratus*
8	*delapan*	200	*duaratus*
9	*sembilan*	300	*tigaratus*
10	*sepuluh*	1000	*seribu*
11	*sebelas*	2000	*duaribu*
12	*duabelas*	3000	*tigaribu*
13	*tigabelas*	1 million	*sejuta*
14	*empatbelas*	2 million	*dua juta*
15	*limabelas*		
16	*enambelas*		
17	*tujuhbelas*		
18	*delapanbelas*		

268   *duaratus enampuluh delapan*
51,783   *limapuluhsaturibu, tujuhratus*
                            delapanpuluh tiga

Fractions

½   *setengah*
⅓   *sepertiga*
¼   *seperempat*
¾   *tiga per empat*

Ordinal Numbers

1st	*pertama*
2nd	*kedua*
3rd	*ketiga*
4th	*keempat*
5th	*kelima*
6th	*keenam*
7th	*ketujuh*
8th	*kedelapan*
9th	*kesembilan*
10th	*kesepuluh*

the first bus	*bis pertama*
the third building	*gedung ketiga*

Quantity

about	*kira-kira*
a little (amount)	*sedikit*
to count	*menghitung*
double	*dobel*
a dozen	*selusin*
enough	*cukup*
few	*sedikit*
many	*banyak*
minus	*kurang*
more	*lagi*
number	*nomer*
one more	*satu lagi*
plus	*tambah*
a pair	*sepasang*

percent	*persen*
quantity	*jumlah*
too (expensive)	*terlalu (mahal)*

Bahasa Indonesia & Bahasa Malaysia

Although the national languages of Indonesia and Malaysia are both based on the same language, known as Malay, the languages have diverged and are developing in somewhat different directions. Many traditional Malay words are falling out of use in Indonesia and are being replaced or supplemented by new words borrowed from Javanese and English, amongst other sources.

You will find, however, that your knowledge of Bahasa Indonesia will form a good basis for travelling in Malaysia and learning Malaysia's language.

The structures and grammars remain common to both languages – the differences are in vocabulary. Unfortunately the different vocabularies include many commonly used words which crop up in many sentences. In most cases your Bahasa Indonesia will be well understood and will probably just be considered a source of amusement. The following are some of the most prominent differences between modern Bahasa Malaysia and Bahasa Indonesia. Many of these differences are not reflected in dictionaries of the languages, but are different in common usage.

English	Indonesian	Malaysian
aeroplane	*pesawat*	*kapalterbang*
after	*sesudah*	*selepas*
afternoon	*sore*	*petang*
always	*selalu*	*sentiasa*
beef	*daging sapi*	*daging lembu*
brother	*saudara*	*abang*

car	*mobil*	*kereta*
city	*kota*	*bandar*
clever	*pintar*	*pandai*
cold (adj)	*dingin*	*sejuk*
cute (baby)	*lucu*	*manis*
delicious	*enak*	*sedap*
fetch someone	*menjemput*	*mengambil*
friend	*teman*	*kawan*
hour of the day	*jam ...*	*pukul ...*
to invite	*mengundang*	*menjemput*
marry	*menikah*	*kawin*
meet	*bertemu*	*berjumpa*
Mr (formal)	*Bapak*	*Tuan*
Mrs (formal)	*Ibu*	*Puan*
office	*kantor*	*pejabat*
petrol	*bensin*	*petrol*
return	*kembali*	*balik*
room	*kamar*	*bilik*
shoes	*sepatu*	*kasut*
shop	*toko*	*kedai*
soon	*sebentar*	*sekejap*
speak	*berbicara*	*bercakap*
staff	*pegawai*	*kakitangan*
Sunday	*Hari Minggu*	*Hari Ahad*
toilet	*WC, kamar kecil*	*tandas*
understand	*mengerti*	*faham*
village	*desa*	*kampung*

Vocabulary

A

above – *diatas*
accident – *kecelakaan*
accompany – *menemani*
acknowledge – *mengakui*
actually – *sebenarnya*
address – *alamat*
adult – *orang dewasa*
advice – *nasehat*
aerogram – *aerogram*
aeroplane – *pesawat*
afraid – *takut*
after – *sesudah*
afternoon – *sore*
again – *sekali lagi*
age – *umur*
agent – *agen*
ago – *yang lalu*
agree – *setuju*
agriculture – *pertanian*
airmail – *pos udara*
airport – *lapangan terbang*
alive – *hidup*
all – *semua*
allergic – *alergi*
alley – *gang*
already – *sudah*

also – *juga*
always – *selalu*
among – *antara*
and – *dan*
angry – *marah*
animal – *binatang*
answer (v) – *jawab* (root word)
— *menjawab* (active verb)
ant – *semut*
antibiotics – *antibiotik*
anything – *apa saja*
anytime – *kapan saja*
anywhere – *dimana saja*
apple – *apel*
approximately – *kira-kira*
arm – *lengan*
arrive – *datang*
artist – *seniman*
ashamed – *malu*
ashtray – *asbak*
ask (v) – *tanya* (root word)
— *bertanya* (active verb)
asleep – *tidur*
assist – *bantu* (root word)
— *membantu* (active verb)

assistance – *bantuan*
at – *di*

B

baby – *bayi*
babysitter – *pramusiwi*
bad – *jahat*
bag – *tas*
baggage – *barang-barang*
ballpoint pen – *pena bolpoin*
banana – *pisang*
bank – *bank*
bank draft – *surat wesel*
bank clerk – *pegawai bank*
barber – *tukang cukur*
bargain (v) – *tawar-menawar*
basket – *keranjang*
bathe – *mandi*
bathroom – *kamar mandi*
beach – *pantai*
beans – *buncis*
beautiful (scenery) – *indah*
beautiful (woman) – *cantik*
because – *karena*
bed – *tempat tidur*
beef – *daging sapi*
beer – *bir*
before – *sebelum*
behind – *di belakang*
better – *lebih baik*
between – *antara*

bicycle – *sepeda*
big – *besar*
bill (money) – *uang kertas*
bill – *bon, rekening*
bird – *burung*
black – *hitam*
blanket – *selimut*
bleed – *berdarah*
blood – *darah*
blue – *biru*
board (n) – *papan*
boat – *perahu*
boil – *merebus*
boiled egg – *telur rebus*
boiled water – *air putih (air rebus)*
bone – *tulang*
book – *buku*
bookshop – *toko buku*
border – *perbatasan*
bored – *bosan*
both – *keduanya*
bottle – *botol*
bottle opener – *alat pembuka botol*
boy – *anak laki-laki*
brain – *otak*
branch (office) – *cabang*
bread – *roti*
break – *pecah*
breakfast – *makan pagi*
breath – *nafas*

bridge – *jembatan*
broken – *patah*
broom – *sapu*
brother – *saudara*
brown – *coklat*
building – *bangunan*
burn – *bakar*
bus station – *stasiun, terminal bis*
bus – *bis*
businessperson – *pengusaha*
busy (location) – *ramai*
but – *tetapi*
butter – *mentega*
buttons – *kancing*
buy – *beli* (root word)
    – *membeli* (active verb)

C

cabbage – *kol*
cabin – *ruang*
cake – *kue*
calm – *tenang*
camera – *kamera*
camp (v) – *kemah* (root word)
    – *berkemah* (active verb)
candle – *lilin*
can opener – *alat pembuka kaleng*
car – *mobil*

careful – *hati-hati*
cash – *uang tunai*
cat – *kucing*
cave – *gua*
chair – *kursi*
change (v) – *ganti* (root word)
    – *mengganti* (active verb)
cheap – *murah*
chemist – *apotik*
cheque – *cek*
chicken – *ayam*
child – *anak*
children – *anak-anak*
chilli – *cabe*
chocolate – *coklat*
cholera – *kolera*
cigarettes – *rokok*
cinema – *bioskop*
city – *kota besar*
clean (adj) – *bersih*
clean (v) – *bersih* (root word)
    – *membersihkan* (active verb)
clear, understood – *jelas*
climb (v) – *naik*
closed – *tutup*
clothing – *pakaian*
cloudy – *mendung*
coconut – *kelapa*
coffee – *kopi*
coins – *uang logam*

cold (sickness) – *sakit selesma*
cold – *dingin*
colour – *warna*
comb – *sisir*
come – *datang*
commission – *komisi*
complain – *mengeluh*
concert – *konser*
condom – *kondom*
confirmation – *penegasan*
constipation – *sembelit*
cook (v) – *masak*
cordial – *sirup*
corner – *sudut*
cost (object) – *harga*
cost (service) – *ongkos*
cough (v) – *batuk*
count – *hitung*
country – *negara*
cow – *sapi*
crab – *kepiting*
cremation – *pembakaran mayat*
crossroad – *perempatan*
crowded – *ramai*
cucumber – *timun*
cup – *cangkir*

D

dangerous – *bahaya*
dark – *gelap*

date – *tanggal*
day – *hari*
day after tomorrow – *lusa*
deforestation – *penebangan hutan*
delicious – *enak*
dentist – *dokter gigi*
depart – *berangkat*
deposit (luggage) – *titip* (root word)
 – *menitipkan* (active verb)
develop (film) – *mencuci*
diarrhoea – *berak berak*
dictionary – *kamus*
different – *berbeda*
difficult – *sukar*
dinner – *makan malam*
dirty – *kotor*
discount – *korting*
disease – *penyakit*
dive (v) – *selam* (root word)
 – *menyelam* (active verb)
do – *buat*
doctor – *dokter*
dog – *anjing*
door – *pintu*
drink – *minum*
driver's licence – *SIM, Surat Ijin Mengemudi*
drop – *jatuh*

drug store – *toko obat*
dry (adj) – *kering*
dry (v) – *jemur* (root word)
    – *menjemur* (active
       verb)
duck – *bebek*
during – *selama*
dust – *debu*
duty – *tugas*
dysentery – *disenteri*

every – *masing-masing*
everybody – *semua orang*
everything – *segala sesuatu*
example – *contoh*
excuse – *alasan*
excuse me – *permisi*
expensive – *mahal*
experience – *pengalaman*
export (v) – *mengekspor*
eye – *mata*

E

each – *tiap-tiap*
ear – *telinga*
early – *pagi-pagi*
east – *timur*
easy – *mudah*
eat – *makan*
economic – *ekonomi*
education – *pendidikan*
egg – *telur*
electricity – *listrik*
embassy – *kedutaan*
emergency – *darurat*
empty (adj) – *kosong*
endorsement – *pengesahan*
engineer – *insinyur*
enough – *cukup*
entrance – *masuk*
envelope – *amplop*
essential – *perlu*

F

face – *muka*
factory – *pabrik*
family – *keluarga*
fan – *kipas*
far – *jauh*
farmer – *petani*
fast (adj) – *cepat*
fast (n, v) – *puasa*
father – *bapak*
fever – *demam*
few – *beberapa*
film – *film*
finger – *jari*
finished – *habis*
fish (n) – *ikan*
fish (v) – *memancing*
flashlight (torch) – *senter*
flour – *tepung*
flower – *bunga*

floor lanteh

follow – *ikut*
food – *makanan*
food stall – *warung*
foot – *kaki*
for – *untuk*
foreign – *asing*
foreigner – *orang asing*
forest – *hutan*
fork – *garpu*
fresh (food) – *segar*
fried – *goreng*
friend – *teman*
frog – *kodok*
from – *dari*
front – *depan*
fruit – *buah-buahan*

glue – *lem*
goat – *kambing*
gold – *mas*
good – *bagus*
goodbye – *selamat jalan*
government – *pemerintah*
grammar – *tatabahasa*
grape – *anggur*
grass – *rumput*
green – *hijau*
ground – *tanah*
group – *kelompok*
guest – *tamu*

G

game – *mainan*
garden – *kebun*
garlic – *bawang*
gentle – *lembut*
geography – *ilmu bumi*
giant – *raksasa*
gift – *hadiah*
girl – *perempuan*
give – *beri* (root word)
     – *memberi* (active verb)
glad – *senang*
glass – *gelas*
glasses (eye) – *kaca mata*

impatient di tak sabar

H

habit – *kebiasaan*
hair – *rambut*
half – *setengah*
hand – *tangan*
handsome (male) – *tampan*
happy – *gembira*
harbour – *pelabuhan*
hard – *keras*
hat – *topi*
head – *kepala*
headache – *sakit kepala*
health – *kesehatan*
hear – *dengar*
heart – *jantung*
heat – *kepanasan*
heavy – *berat*
help – *tolong*
here – *disini*
high – *tinggi*
hill – *bukit*
hire/rent – *sewa*
historical ruins – *runtuhan*
history – *sejarah*
hole – *lobang*
holiday – *liburan*
honest – *terus terang*
horn – *tanduk*
horse – *kuda*
hospital – *rumah sakit*
hot – *panas*

hot (spicy) – *pedas*
hour – *jam*
how – *bagaimana*
how much – *berapa*
humid – *lembab*
hungry – *lapar*
hunt (v) – *berburu*
husband – *suami*

I

I – *saya, aku*
ice cream – *es krim*
ice – *es*
idea – *ide*
identification – *surat keterangan*
if – *kalau*
imagine – *membayangkan*
immediately – *dengan segara*
indigenous – *asli*
infection – *infeksi*
information – *keterangan*
injection – *suntikan*
insect – *serangga*
inside – *didalam*
insurance – *asuransi*
interesting – *menarik*
intersection – *persimpangan*
island – *pulau*
itch – *gatal*
ivory – *gading*

J

jacket – *jaket*
jackfruit – *nangka*
jail – *penjara*
jar – *toples*
jealous – *iri hati*
jewellery – *intan permata*
job – *pekerjaan*
journalist – *wartawan*
jump – *lompat*
just – *baru*
just one – *satu saja*
justice – *keadilan*

K

key – *kunci*
kiss – *cium* (root word)
   – *mencium* (active verb)
kitchen – *dapur*
knife – *pisau*
know (v) – *tahu*

L

lake – *danau*
lamb – *domba*
land – *tanah*
landscape – *pemandangan*

language – *bahasa*
last – *terakhir*
late – *terlambat*
later – *nanti*
laugh – *tertawa*
law – *hukum*
lawyer – *ahli hukum*
lay down – *berbaring*
leak – *bocor*
leather – *kulit*
lecture – *kuliah*
lecturer – *dosen*
left (opposite of right) – *kiri*
leg – *kaki*
lemon – *jeruk asam*
length – *panjang*
letter – *surat*
lice – *kutu*
life – *hidup*
light (adj) – *ringan*
light (n) – *lampu*
like (v) – *suka*
little, a – *sedikit*
live (exist/dwell) – *tinggal*
liver – *hati*
lock – *kunci*
long (measure) – *panjang*
long (time) – *lama*
look – *lihat*
lost – *tersesat*
lotion – *cairan*
lounge (room) – *ruang tamu*

lightening   Puter.

love – *kasih, cinta*
luck – *untung*
lunch – *makan siang*

M

mad – *gila*
magazine – *majalah*
main – *utama*
make (v) – *buat* (root word)
– *membuat* (active verb)
malaria – *malaria*
male – *laki-laki*
man – *orang laki-laki*
mango – *mangga*
many – *banyak*
map – *peta*
marry – *menikah* (polite), *kawin*
market – *pasar*
mask – *topeng*
matches – *korek api*
material – *kain*
mattress – *kasur*
may – *boleh*
meaning – *makna*
meat – *daging*
medicine – *obat-obat*
meet – *bertemu*
menu – *daftar makanan*

message – *pesan*
milk – *susu*
mineral water – *Aqua, air soda*
minute – *menit*
mirror – *cermin*
Miss – *Nona*
mistake – *salah*
misunderstanding – *salah paham*
money – *uang*
monkey – *kera*
month – *bulan*
more – *lagi*
morning – *pagi*
Moslem – *orang Islam*
mosque – *mesjid*
mosquito – *nyamuk*
mosquito net – *kelambu*
most (the) – *paling*
mother – *ibu*
motorcycle – *sepeda motor*
mountain – *gunung*
Mr – *Bapak*
Mrs – *Nyonya*
much – *banyak*
mud – *lumpur*
museum – *musium*
music – *musik*
must – *harus*
mutton – *daging domba*

N

name – *nama*
napkin – *serbet*
nationality – *kebangsaan*
near – *dekat*
necessary – *perlu*
need – *perlu*
neighbour – *tetangga*
nervous – *gelisah*
never – *tak pernah*
never mind – *tidak apa-apa*
new – *baru*
newspaper – *koran*
nice – *bagus*
night – *malam*
no, not – *tidak*
noisy – *bising*
noodles – *mie*
north – *utara*
nose – *hidung*
not yet – *belum*
now – *sekarang*
nude – *telanjang*
number – *nomor*
nurse – *jururawat*
nut – *kacang*

O

object – *benda*
occupation – *pekerjaan*

ocean – *laut*
odd – *aneh*
offer – *tawaran*
office – *kantor*
often – *sering*
old – *tua*
older brother – *abang*
older sister – *kakak*
once – *satu kali*
onion – *bawang*
only – *hanya*
open – *buka*
operation – *operasi*
or – *atau*
orange – *jeruk manis*
over here – *disini*
over there – *disana*
owe – *berhutang*

P

pain – *sakit*
paintings – *lukisan*
paper – *kertas*
parcel – *paket, bungkus*
park – *taman*
park (v) – *parkir*
pawpaw – *papaya*
pay (v) – *bayar* (root word)
        – *membayar* (active
                verb)
peanut – *kacang*

pen – *pena*
penalty – *hukuman*
pepper – *lada*
percent – *persen*
perhaps – *barangkali*
person – *orang*
petrol – *bensin*
pharmacy – *apotik*
photograph – *foto*
picture – *gambar*
pig – *babi*
pillow – *bantal*
pineapple – *nanas, nenas*
place – *tempat*
plane – *pesawat terbang*
plant (n) – *tanaman*
plate – *piring*
please – *silakan/tolong*
plus – *tambah*
poisonous – *beracun*
police – *polisi*
poor – *miskin*
pork – *daging babi*
possibly – *mungkin*
post office – *kantor pos*
postage – *bea*
postcard – *kartu pos*
pot (cooking) – *panci*
potato – *kentang*
prefer (v) – *lebih suka*
pregnant – *hamil*
prescription – *resep*

problem – *masalah*
profession – *pekerjaan*
pull – *menarik*
puppets – *wayang kulit*
push – *dorong* (root word)
– *mendorong* (active verb)

Q

quality – *kwalitas*
quantity – *jumlah*
question – *pertanyaan*
quickly – *cepat*
quiet – *tenang*
quinine – *kina*

R

rain – *hujan*
razor – *alat cukur*
read – *membaca*
ready – *siap*
receipt – *kwitansi*
receive – *menerima*
red – *merah*
reforestation – *reboisasi*
refrigerator – *lemari es*
refuse (v) – *tolak* (root word)
    – *menolak* (active
    verb)
region – *wilayah*
religion – *agama*
remember – *ingat*
rent (v) – *sewa* (root word)
    – *menyewa* (active
    verb)
repair – *memperbaiki*
repeat – *mengulangi*
reply – *jawaban*
request (v) – *minta*
reservation – *pesanan tempat*
respect – *hormat*
responsibility – *tanggung
jawab*
restaurant – *rumah makan,
restoran*
return – *kembali*
rheumatism – *encok*

rice – *nasi*
rich – *kaya*
right (correct) – *benar*
right (opposite of left) – *kanan*
ring – *cincin*
ripe – *matang*
river – *sungai*
road – *jalan*
roasted – *panggang*
rock – *batu*
roof – *atap*
room – *kamar*
rope – *tampar, tali*
rotten – *busuk*
round – *bulat*
rubbish – *sampah*
run – *lari*

S

sail – *layar*
sailor – *pelaut*
salt – *garam*
salty – *asin*
same – *sama-sama*
sand – *pasir*
sandals – *sandal*
scared – *takut*
scenery – *pemandangan*
school – *sekolah*
sea – *laut*
season – *musim*

seat – *tempat duduk*
seat belt – *sabuk*
second (unit of time) – *detik*
see – *lihat*
seldom – *jarang*
sell – *jual*
send (v) – *kirim* (root word)
       – *mengirim* (active
             verb)
sentence – *kalimat*
servant – *pembantu*
service – *pelayanan*
service charge – *ongkos*
sew – *jahit*
shade – *teduh*
shampoo (n) – *sampo*
shampoo (v) – *keramas*
shave – *cukur*
sheet (bed) – *seprei*
shells – *batok*
ship – *kapal*
shoelaces – *tali sepatu*
shop – *toko*
shrimp – *udang*
shut – *tutup*
sick – *sakit*
signature – *tandatangan*
silver – *perak*
since – *sejak*
singer – *penyanyi*
sister – *saudara*
sit – *duduk*

skin – *kulit*
sleep – *tidur*
sleeping bag – *tas tidur*
slow – *pelan*
small – *kecil*
smell – *mencium*
snake – *ular*
soap – *sabun*
socks – *kaos kaki*
soft – *lembut*
some – *beberapa*
sometimes – *kadang-kadang*
son – *anak laki-laki*
song – *lagu*
sorry – *maaf*
sour – *asam*
south – *selatan*
soy sauce – *kecap asin*
speak – *bicara*
spicy – *pedas*
spoon – *sendok*
stairs – *tangga*
stale – *lama*
stamp – *perangko*
starfruit – *belimbing*
stationmaster – *kepala stasiun*
stomach – *perut*
stomachache – *sakit perut*
stone – *batu*
stop! – *stop!*
strange – *aneh*
street – *jalan*

strong   kuat

student – *pelajar*
style – *gaya*
sugar – *gula*
suitcase – *kopor*
sun – *mata hari*
sunburnt – *kulit terbakar*
surface mail – *pos biasa*
sweet (adj) – *manis*
sweets – *gula-gula*
swim (v) – *renang* (root word)
            – *berenang* (active
                  verb)
swimsuit – *baju renang*

T

table – *meja*
tablet – *tablet*
tailor – *penjahit*
take off (depart) – *berangkat*
tampons – *tampon*
taste – *rasa*
tax – *pajak*
taxi – *taksi*
tea – *teh*
teacher – *guru*
teeth – *gigi*
telegram – *kawat*
telephone – *telepon*
television – *televisi*
teller – *kasir*
temple – *candi*

tent – *tenda*
thank you – *terima kasih*
that – *itu*
theatre – *gedung sandiwara*
there is – *ada*
they – *mereka*
thirsty – *haus*
this – *ini*
thread – *benang*
throat – *tenggorokan*
ticket – *karcis*
ticket window – *loket*
tiger – *harimau*
tight – *sempit*
timetable – *daftar*
tired – *lelah*
to – *ke*
today – *hari ini*
toilet paper – *kertas kamar
  kecil*
toilet – *kamar kecil*
tomorrow – *besok*
tongue – *lidah*
too – *terlalu*
tool – *alat*
tooth – *gigi*
toothbrush – *sikat gigi*
torch (flashlight) – *senter*
touch – *sentuh*
tourist – *turis*
towel – *handuk*
train – *kereta api*

travel – *jalan-jalan*
travellers' cheque – *cek turis*
tree – *pohon*
truck – *truk*
true – *benar*
turn – *belok*
typhoid – *demam tipus*

U

umbrella – *payung*
under – *dibawah*
understand (v) – *mengerti*
underwear – *pakaian dalam*
unemployment – *pengang-
  guran*
university – *universitas*
unripe – *mentah*

V

valley – *lembah*
vegetables – *sayur-sayuran*
very – *sangat*
village – *desa*
volcano – *gunung api*
vomit – *muntah*
vulgar – *kasar*

W

wait – *tunggu*

waiter – *pelayan*
wake up – *bangun*
walk – *jalan kaki*
wall – *dinding*
want (v) – *mau*
warm – *hangat*
wash – *cuci*
Watch out! – *Hati-hati!*
water – *air*
  boiled water – *air rebus*
  purified water – *air putih*
waterfall – *air terjun*
watermelon – *semangka*
waves – *ombak*
we – *kami, kita*
weather – *cuaca*
week – *minggu*
weigh (v) – *timbang* (root word)
       – *menimbang* (active
          verb)
west – *barat*
wet – *basah*
what – *apa*
wheel – *roda*
When? – *Kapan?*
Where? – *Di mana?*
which – *yang mana*
white – *putih*
Who? – *Siapa?*
whole – *penuh*
Why? – *Mengapa?*
wife – *istri*

wind – *angin*
window – *jendela*
wine – *anggur*
with – *dengan*
without – *tanpa*
woman – *perempuan*
wood (timber) – *kayu*
woodcarving – *ukiran kayu*
wool – *bulu*
word – *kata*
world – *bumi*
writer – *penulis*
writing paper – *kertas tulis*

Y

year – *tahun*
yellow – *kuning*
yes – *ya*
yesterday – *kemarin*
yield – *hasil*
you – *saudara, anda*
young – *muda*

Z

zoo – *kebun binatang*

weak - lelah

- ANDI ZAINAL
- BUDI KASEH.
* TUAN SIM.

Emergencies

Help!	*Tolong!*
It's an emergency!	*Keadaan darurat!*
There's been an accident!	*Ada kecelakaan!*
Call a doctor!	*Panggil dokter!*
Call an ambulance!	*Panggil ambulan!*
I've been robbed!	*Saya dirampok!*
Stop!	*Stop!*
Go away!	*Pergi!*
I'll get the police!	*Saya akan panggil polisi!*
Watch out!	*Awas!*
Thief!	*Copet!*
Fire!	*Kebakaran!*

I've lost ...   *Saya kehilangan ...*
    my bag   *tas saya*
    my money   *uang saya*
    my travellers' cheque   *cek wisata saya*
    my passport   *paspor saya*

I am ill.	*Saya sakit.*
I am lost.	*Saya tersesat.*
Where is the police station?	*Dimana ada kantor polisi?*
Where are the toilets?	*Dimana ada WC?*

Could you help me please?	*Boleh minta tolong?*
Could I please use the telephone?	*Boleh saya pakai telepon?*
I wish to contact my embassy/consulate.	*Saya mau menghubungi kedutaan besar/konsulat saya.*
I speak English.	*Saya berbahasa Inggris.*
I have medical insurance.	*Saya punya asuransi kesehatan.*
I understand.	*Saya mengerti.*
I don't understand.	*Saya tidak mengerti.*
I didn't realize that I was doing anything wrong.	*Saya tidak tahu kalau saya salah.*
I didn't do it.	*Saya tidak melakukan itu.*
I'm sorry. I apologise.	*Saya minta maaf.*
My contact number (next of kin)	*Nomor kontak saya (saudara dekat)*
My blood group is ...	*Golongan darah saya ...*
(A, B, O, AB) positive/ negative	*(A, B, O, AB) positif/negatif*

Handwritten notes:

Bali Mabuyck Gich   12/12

PUTU : SUDIT
JLN. CEMPAKA, K.LK -
KALIBUKBUK LOVINA
BALI
INDONESIA

Bali & Lombok
a travel survival kit

This guide will help travellers to experience the real magic of Bali's tropical paradise. Neighbouring Lombok is largely untouched by outside influences and has a special atmosphere of its own.

Indonesia
a travel survival kit

Some of the most remarkable sights and sounds in South-East Asia can be found amongst the 7000 islands of Indonesia – this book covers the entire archipelago in detail.